Telling a Hawk from a Handsaw

CHRIS WALLACE-CRABBE was born in 1934. After graduating in English, he became Lockie Fellow in Australian Literature and Creative Writing, Melbourne University, from 1961 to 1963, and over the next decades he became Reader in English and then held a Personal Chair from 1988. He was Harkness Fellow at Yale University 1965–7, Professor of Australian Studies at Harvard, 1987–8, and visiting Professor at the University of Venice, 1973 and 2005. His first book of poems was published in Australia in 1959, but in the 1980s he began to publish with Oxford University Press, with *The Amorous Cannibal*. His most recent books of verse include *By and Large* (2001), *The Universe Looks Down* (Brandl and Schlesinger, 2005) and the bilingual *Each Line of Writing Still Is to be Done* (L'Officina, 2006). *Read It Again*, a volume of critical essays, was published by Salt in 2005. Chris Wallace-Crabbe has given many readings of his poetry around the world, and chairs the newly established Australian Poetry Centre in St Kilda, Victoria. Also a commentator on the visual arts, he specialises in artists' books. Among other awards, he has won the Dublin Prize for Arts and Sciences and the Christopher Brennan Award for Literature. Since his retirement he has been Professor Emeritus in the Australian Centre, the University of Melbourne.

Also by Chris Wallace-Crabbe from Carcanet Press / OxfordPoets

Selected Poems
By and Large

CHRIS WALLACE-CRABBE

Telling a Hawk from a Handsaw

Oxford*Poets*

CARCANET

First published in Great Britain in 2008 by
Carcanet Press Limited
Alliance House
Cross Street
Manchester M2 7AQ

A CIP catalogue record for this book is available from the British Library
ISBN 978 1 903039 93 9

The publisher acknowledges financial assistance from Arts Council England

Typeset in Bembo by XL Publishing Services, Tiverton
Printed and bound in England by SRP Ltd, Exeter

For Kristin

So in the future, the sister of the past, I may see myself as I sit here now but by reflection from that which I then shall be.
James Joyce

Acknowledgements

Some of these poems first appeared in the following journals and magazines:

The Age, Agenda, Antipodes, Australian Book Review, Eureka Street, Harvard Review, Heat, Island, Jacket, Kunapipi, The London Magazine, Meanjin, Notre Dame Review, Overland, PN Review, Poetry Ireland Review, Poetry Review, PAN, Poetry Porch, Southerly, Verse, Warwick Review, Westerly, Yale Review.

Also in *The Forward Book of Poetry* (2002; Faber), *Vintage: Celebrating Ten Years of the Mildura Writers' Festival* (2004; Hardie Grant Books), *Said the Rat! Writers at the Water Rat 2000–2003* (2003; Black Pepper), *Still Shines When You Think of It: A Festschrift for Vincent O'Sullivan* (2007; Victoria University Press), *The Best Australian Poems* (2004, 2005; Black Inc.) and *Best Australian Poetry* (2004, 2005, 2006; University of Queensland Press). A number of poems appeared in small chapbooks from my own Gungurru Press: *A Representative Human, Next,* and *Then*.

Many pieces here were produced while I was enjoying a most welcome New Work grant from the Literature Board of the Australia Council. Then again, some were written during a residency at Bundanon Artists' Retreat, for which I want to express my gratitude, as I do to the Australian Centre, University of Melbourne, where I do much of my writing.

Contents

A Vocation	9
And Terror	11
Gross and Violent Stimulants	12
It Sounds Different Today	13
The Domestic Sublime:	
The Surface of Things	15
Saucer	15
Indoor Yachting	16
Coat Hangers Galore	16
Garlic	17
At the Clothesline	17
Its Private Idiom	18
The Alignments	19
Ending with a Preposition	22
Theogony	23
From the Island, Bundanon	24
Mitsubishi Moments	27
Daphne Fitzroy	28
Delivering Tact	29
Along the Bough	30
Joy on the Very Edge of History	31
Grasses	33
And Gathering Swallows Twitter	34
Anne Miller	35
Our Birth is but a Sleep and a Forgetting	37
The Speech of Birds	38
At the Bionic Elephant	39
Do I Sleep or Am I Slept?	41
A Faun's Arvo	42
Meanings of Lowell	43
Near the Ha-Ha, Bundanon	45
Leaning Against the Golden Undertow	46
Intermezzo	47
Parking for Zeno	49
The Stone's in the Midst of All	50
A Descendant	51
One Step after Another	53
Reading Smoke with Orpheus	54

Provincial Distinctions   56
Boleyn, Tourist   57
Mozart on the Road   58
The Drudges   60
A Triptych for my Father   61
Not Going to Korea After All   63
The World as Will and Idea   64
A Summons in the Peak Period   65
Stranger Country   66
The Land of Motionless Childhood   67
Loving in Truth   69
Oh Yes, Then   70
We Are All Grown-ups   71

A Vocation

for Peter Porter

The burden I have carried through the world
is having been expected to be happy,
true friends imagining that I could
crack my jokes to the tune of 'Auld Lang Syne'
while I went on splitting wagonloads of firewood.

My particular joke was being healthy
but many of you have done the dirty on me,
slipping away to death: I am displeased
at so many fellows giving up like that.
The life-spirit demands we call them back

but in the long run this may be no more
than the dram of D.II. Lawrence deep inside me,
romantic as a thistle or a snake
swaggering that I'm On the Side of Life,
suntanned here in the lost antipodes

of childhood's yellow beach and glaucous water.
The dream of me has grown up with its dream
becoming the words it took delight in hearing,
canny phrases from Kipling or R.L.S.:
just murmuring them can make a bloke survive,

or that's my solar myth. It must be something
to have grown beyond the fear of melanoma
and its grim fellows. My birdsong world keeps ringing
with lots of tiresome jobs that must be done.
Perhaps I'm a battler, yet my aunt said,

'We don't want any battlers in our family.'
Aunty was tough as the brown camouflage netting
she taught me how to make against the Jap
when life was all composed of doing things:
I guess I'm not the type for meditation

and yet can boast as many snips of thought
as any nerd chained to his VDU.
When I enter some room I carry with me
voices from outside the cemetery
and the rich verbal memory of sweat:

the myth I keep on peddling through a life,
that work may be identical with play,
will do me after all. We don't have many lives.
Grasping my bunch of keys I turn the rusty lock and
stroll among the values that are mine.

And Terror

When the two liberal centuries –
    intermittently, that is
    and far from everywhere –
came to their carefully
choreographed end

we found ourselves
translated way back into
the gritty libretti
of Joseph Conrad, very best
Polish writer in the language.

Those over-busy ugly airports
made us take off our belts and shoes,
et cetera, while the daily papers
filled out with young men bearing
exotic names.

Some of them even came
from cricketing countries.
We were bound to applaud
two empty signifiers now:
security and terror.

Gross and Violent Stimulants

Back here, at undawn or piccaninny daylight
you roll over grumpy
working out what to do
with the usual intrusive elbow.

Waking early to doves
and hypnopompic diction
one mutters, 'Latifundia',
or 'drizzle with olive oil'.

Toward the dot of setting Venus
early sparrows,
dusty little toughs
try out a note or two;

if the news is bad
then it's called news
but if not,
not.

Terror! But terror is a clumsy
over-usable noun
we learned once when hearing about
the Stern Gang

and its dimensions
have now
blown out of mind
completely.

It Sounds Different Today

How far can it matter to 'god' or to
the human race, let alone this planet

whether you notice how far the dry valley has
turned silvery when you opened your sunned eyes;

again, if you noticed that fade-red MG, or
how accurately words can set down the sight

of a digging wombat hurling up brown clods
of burrow-earth? We must have been set down

here to do something or other well, but then
who or what is ever going to remember that,

you ask yourself, taking an epicurean nap.
No deadlines this week, nothing to do for

odd students, nor for the undulating network
family means; next in the scale would come the

Persian carpet of history, in which there just
might be a dint or digit that remembered your

being here – for say a century, or several
until the whole circus had been burned off

the road, costumes, clown and performing bears
including the human race, as it might have been.

Come to that, when you take good note
of the way plural midday sunlight glances back

brassily from the upper leaves of those spotted gums
or jot down the names you most frequently forget,

it is absurdly being done for some project which
we may as well name god: ironically put together

from the Ikea kits of personal consciousness,
those private dillybags that could well include

cataracts, PMT, envy, Protestantism and all.
You pick up your old box of coloured pencils and start again.

The Domestic Sublime

My dears, my dears, I say to the plates and the spoons.

Iris Murdoch

The Surface of Things

Pleasantly rolling deodorant into an oxter
    He thought of the shave ahead,
Whether to start in the upper left-hand corner
    Or the slant of his jaw instead.

From the loose aggregate of these choices
    A common life is made,
Fate no more than a thicket of brand-names
    And the moment when you delayed.

Saucer

who first spotted the lack
not that is the slip
in between the cup and lip
but down under a hot mug
              or cup?
yet if it comes to that
a plate would merely be over the top

something then to stop the drips
or keep the pea soup off your lap
complicate the washing up
stop a simple splash
             or slop
and sit here for the waiter's tip

sad without a cup

Indoor Yachting

Has any mere scribbler
ever spotted or caught

that fine dramatic gesture
by which a homebody

standing down at the bed-end
flourishes a wide clean sheet and

blows it out like a spinnaker
so that the far end

will flutter down in place
where a pillow will be,

once again
getting it right?

Coat Hangers Galore

Clubbable and promiscuous,
                              they hang around
getting under your feet
while always intending to be helpful;

wiry and would-be athletic
they just keep falling into a tangle
putting a foot
                    in somebody else's mouth.

Garlic

Adhesive, papery,
the wan delicate skin
sticks for just a smidgen
too long, until

a naked clove
comes out successfully
shining
virginal as the dawn

yet leaving
its ripe sex on your fingers
for quite some time.

At the Clothesline

What I'd thought a fallen shirt
Under the line, flat on the grass
Was nothing but my shadow there,
Hinting that all things pass:

That many we loved or used to know
Are dragged already out of sight,
Vanished fast, though stepping slow,
Folded into remorseless night.

My dark trace now has quit the lawn.
Everything slips away too soon,
Yet something leaves its mark here like
A rainbow ring around the moon.

Its Private Idiom

A room lies open
giving onto grasscoloured silence,
the racket of our footsteps gone away

and the dust
which is friend to mankind
gathers over every thing inside

so that
when blue sky peeps in at breakfast-time
it sees the kindly coverlet of dust

like blessing
or a grey army blanket.

Sweet dust, bless us all in turn.

Keep us warm, if you can,
poor in our openness.

The Alignments

A dot
has only one direction,
    a line has two,
or so we were taught at school
back in the short pants and gravel days
long before particle physics.

★

Tell me, please,
    which way
did Time go?
        I'd love to know.

★

And early on
as a child-metaphysician,
my daughter up and queried it all:
    'Why do things
    have a line around them?'
She ought to have tried Wittgenstein.

★

Just making it longer and longer, where does it get you?

★

Looking out over
the ocean's long inhuman reticence,
what rhythmical alternatives,
what miles of diamonds!

★

Toward orange sunset
on the grass-dry plain
I stare stupidly at silvery railway lines,
thinking they meet near infinity.

*

Making the slow line dip and sway in its motion
proceeding gravely into and out of the limelight
is worth the endeavour, if you are given to word-games,

which all of us are in one way or another,
playing at words of love and the diction of dying,
what we say being just as green as the world is.

*

Why is our writing all made up of lines?
There must be something capillary about signs:
look how the envious ink uncoils and twines.

*

Days of reflective Paul Klee!
It was the painter then
            talking of
taking a line for a walk, like a dog,
that really set me off
            on this little track.

*

Dream of a geometer or some architect's draughtsman,
      the beautiful russet sandstone
has been laying down its hairline strata
      as fine as Thomas Bewick ever did
to capture our attention with lineations:
      engraving in three dimensions!

*

Things baffle me,
      solids have turned out so mysterious.
      I think they are the matter
      our dreams were made of,
                  crudely enough

by smiths and naiads
                    in the Silver Age.

                    ★

Following me, old footprints,
you trace a trail
across our imagined map,
mile after dotted mile
far to the nor'-by-northwest,
or so it feels to me.

                    ★

Evening glides silently in
to ask us what
merest reality may be,
any more than, say,
lines and shadows,
shadow and line.

                    ★

Whatever the headlines
in that dawn-thrown morning paper,
some passing snail
has left its own strand
of autobiography
in calligraphy of silver
there,
          across the doorstep.

                    ★

          How short
would a life have to be
for sheer disappointment?

          And how very short
the would-be defining line
that was only a dot in space?

Ending with a Preposition

The news could be hardly new while it becomes

fanatical and faintly luminous
but is life all that different or drear,
something more than a sticky wicket, when
you have let your sub to *The New Yorker* fall away?

Plenitude, the unseen flutefilled magpie
carolling its dulcet fanfaronade,
pleases us, drawing the past to guarantee
a separateness in every living thing,

those lonesome ones constructing society
so as to get food, frock shops and police;
the rich woman's back fence now gone cutely mobile,
readier to say that this will end in tears.

The universe fills up with compensating cartoons,
more tousled cloud rolls in like tumbled blondes,
metaphysics falters yet again, and
extra cover is moved to backward point.

The sprained ankle is hardly where we're at.

Theogony

All jokes
about God
should end with
'I know',

His consciousness
being
a shrewd
cogito.

From the Island, Bundanon

1

Eight stones lie on my trestle desk,
three cream-striped with injected quartzite,
one a very plain grey segment
for the moon goddess, three pebblesized
white, ginger and lustrous black; the last
a pocked palmful of sandstone.

River-rubbed, they fall into design.

2

Muscular underachievers with big brainpans,
Neanderthals dawdled on in the west of Europe
until that corner caught up with the rest of us
then nicked on smartly, ahead for centuries
or more, playing tricks with bright metal and glass.
Where are the old values?
What became of those big blokes and their women?

3

Unknowable, they fall into design,
stars that all peoples have known
by cluster-name, and flowing down the sky
a Milky Way: the whole beyond belief,
altogether impossible
yet across them drags
the flickering of two planes bound for Melbourne.

4

Why is mistletoe so droopingly widespread
in this country,
so far indeed
from Sir J.G. Frazer's multinational magic?
Is it a marsupial kissing-bough
trailing its message of scimitars and bullets
in parody on a parent eucalypt?
The bush is hospitable to such festoons.

5

The rocksolid wombat
that has a dithering habit
neither thunders away
nor gets around to diving
into his well-dug bolthole
but pauses in dusty fur
to consider all the options.

6

Urban *they* remain quite as desiccating
as the dear little sachet of calcium chloride
you find in a chemist's bottle.
They
have no response to the way the lower
squadron of windblown cloud
rushes past us, dynamically indifferent
to the marbled welkin above.

7

Innocent cylinder with a wound,
you have kept the grape's rich blood
from the disillusioning breath of day
at your own cost. Freckled and branded
you lie here on the table,
one end pale magenta. Far from your tree
you became pleasure's sacrifice.

8

Scar tissue earned from shorts and dead lantana
mapping that stony island
has left a cartography of signs
all over both shins, generously so.
Like stars or complicated cells
they look to spell a message I can't read,
inescapably riverine.
And rough.

9

To make, said Hardy, the clock of years
turn backward, I might enter then
a decade when there was my father
and I might know my eldest son
in his plight, but these are dream
as I shuffle the stones on my writing desk
and the stars whirl in endless night.

Mitsubishi Moments

At peak of summer
the paddocks have all turned blonde
    like Toorak mothers.

Those flying foxes
object to the horrid phrase,
    Bats in the belfry.

Humans are not quite
the full sixpence, but can still
    flatter, flirt and charm.

Presence absorbs them
and they do self-expression
    in outdoor cafés.

With large speaking eyes
she hinted she was part of
    these exciting times.

Like avenue elms
green political leaders
    turn out all the same:

one learned from Stalin
the strong magic of changing
    municipal names.

The migrant from Prague
trundles in his wheely bin
    past the limp yucca.

Daphne Fitzroy

A crunch of bearcoloured hair;
the self smallish, bespectacled, in a royalblue blouse
her nose rhymes with her chin's
                    attenuated line.

Pale heartshaped face (nice cheekbones there)
sipping a yellow short drink
                    fortyishly
as she keeps breaking out into
an indrawn laugh
that's impish, an imp would say,
at least winsome
as she pivots fro and to again
between boyfriend and barmaid,
mouth small as a sparrow's.

Light slanting down from the left,
now she fondles
a fancy bottle of crème de cacao
and laughs like a drain
behind her angled, rising cumulus of smoke.

Delivering Tact

At your front gate
        an oily truck murmurs away
patiently enough, it could be said,
while two young blokes
        in tattoos and muddy denims
tug the small heavy sacks up to your house.

They are delivering tact
        and it's expensive
but worth every penny of the cost,
given it makes the whole shebang
        tick along smooth and quiet
like the innards of a bedside clock.

That's right: it lubricates existence.

You take delivery,
        sign a docket
and the truck puffs up white dust.

Locked in a jail of ribs, the passionate heart
judders
        the way a cranked car used to do,
the whole system
                suddenly coughing.

Along the Bough

It is a kind of heat-furred epilogue to wistfulness
when all the lamplike apricots

only last week
throbbing and thronged in their dense trees

have fallen plump away,
sprawl browning on the oddly fruitful concrete

or linger as tantalising survivors
on a skinny branch protected by part-shade.

Straining from the ladder
you just can't quite get out to them

while these last nearer
are gravely blackbird-bitten or else

rotting on the far side,
their damaged hemisphere.

But the taste, the taste of the very best
lingers in your mouth, yes, you are the one

who has eaten sunshine,
swallowing its gorgeous glow.

A year further on they will come to you again,
filling your basket with gladness.

Joy on the Very Edge of History

for Les Murray

How do you write about the condition
of joy? In present participles, I guess.
Not fun, nor merriment, nor yet a state of
optimism: simple joy, persisting
through an afternoon as though the dusty world
has been suddenly cleansed of wheely bins,
of bills, fussing, all shadow of pain or loss.
In a moment of absentminded benignity
St Michael has thrown the gates of Eden open
and the verbs have no direct objects.

Windows give onto sheer pastoral, soothing paddocks
of beige pigmentation and fretwork foliage.
Cloud and drizzle have given over completely.
Over the dark wine we laugh like immortals.
This table is Olympus with a teapot;
while those rainbow lorikeets whistle over,
not bothering at all with orchestration:
it has become the Great Good Place.
A condition like this could be described as erotic,
being a time of spidery grevilleas
in flower, genuine spiderwebs grubbying
the old shed, bees in the lavender hedge
and an old roan munching tussocks.

We are not there but the effect is.
We sit on bent-cane chairs by winking glass,
somewhere bright and early in a century
whose history we can't begin to read.
But, as a slightly national impression,
everybody near at hand is unaccountably
laughing. Our smiles are solar, for a while;
the Shiraz winks at us like a semaphore.
So this is joy, nor am I out of it.
Even the clock with its roman numbering

appears to have forgotten us. And now
the sun like a well-trained border collie
surveys everything from its benign,
low, picturesque angle. Time out.

Grasses

Sternly avoiding the asphalt, treading on grass
I pick my pernickety way across
this common urban transliteration of landscape,
the oddly broadcast parks and median-strips,
saluting the god of grass with the rub of my feet:

feet which are held at bay by animal-skins,
tanned, sewn, polished, and frequently scuffed.
Whitman wrote about your multiplicity
as leaves, and yet those thousands of blades are you,
billions, rather. Bland in your closepacked greenness,

your number exceeds those from whose fate you sprout.
Lushly after rain or wispily blond in summer,
bowing briefly you offer a carpet's welcome
still to the odd walker.
                    Lightly arriving
at a roundabout, I would choose the diagonal,

taking note of kikuyu, buffalo, bent and sedge,
feeling in touch, treading a kind of worship
or else, playing with language, my worship of kind.
Old Whitman thought you the hair of young dead men
but you whisper at my feet
                    that something will survive.

And Gathering Swallows Twitter

for Paul Carter

You might think the world is being taken over
by those properly named rainbow lorikeets
whizzing over like fighter planes that squeal
but a couple of magpies have moved south into our square,
reasserting the musical verities: a square in which
seagulls assemble late every morning
to be fed with crumbled bread by the old Greek woman
next door. Sometimes we see a raven or two
hoeing into dry sandwiches; and feral pigeons,
oddly so-called, given they live in cities,
and not at all in a secretive way like foxes do.
Mudlarks, peculiarly at home with traffic,
are generally called peewits in New South Wales,
although their yelp is far more piercing than that.
Red-rumped or grass parrots will start up under your feet
as you cross the far larger park, where softly spoken doves
and unwelcome starlings are also grazing: Ted Hughes
likened the latter to blowflies. They have a nasty sheen.
Sparrows abound where concrete and crumbs abound,
with a particular fondness for the stylish outdoor café,
while Indian mynahs can well look after themselves.
Wattlebirds are aggressive and lithe: according to Cayley
they produce a sound much like pulling the cork
out from a bottle of wine. At other times
it's the loud repeated effect of a donkey braying.
Once I saw a bloke in nocturnal pyjamas
beating a streetside tree with a furious broom,
attempting to quell the din. Attractive greenies
with their sliver of white carol from treetops
in the most pleasing way, keeping it brief.
All of them belong to a geographical culture
that both underlies and overlays our own,
and will no doubt be glad to be rid of us
in God's good time or that of the ozone layer
or some other card in the genetic casino.

Anne Miller

after Bartok

'Come on out with me, Anne Miller,
Come and follow my rambling,
Follow my free wandering steps
Under the shade of the wonder tree.'

'No, I won't go, reckless Martin.
I'm not going to leave my peaceful house,
My warm house and a gentle husband,
Nor leave my little baby.'

But Anne Miller did go off with him
Into the shade of the wonder tree.
She suddenly stopped and looked above her
Into the boughs of that wonder tree.

Seven women were hanging dead:
Anne Miller burst into crying
And the soldier turned and asked her,
'Why are you weeping, Anne Miller?'

'I'm not weeping, reckless Martin.
Dew keeps dripping from the branches,
And the wonder tree's chilly dewdrops
Keep on wetting my cheeks.'

'Anne, lovely Anne Miller,
Let me look into your eyes.'
Anne Miller stared hard at the soldier
And he fell fast asleep.

She drew out his bright steel sword
And cut the soldier's throat;
She dressed up in his clothing
And set off back toward home.

'Good evening, gentleman farmer,
Can you give me a night's shelter?'
'I'm sorry, good lieutenant, but
My baby's in there crying.'

'Farmer, gentleman farmer,
 Is there good wine here in the village?'
'Yes, a fine tokay, next door.'
'Please get us some for dinner.'

The gentle farmer went for wine,
The soldier took off her greatcoat;
Then she unbuttoned the coarse tunic
And fed her little baby.

Our Birth is but a Sleep and a Forgetting

for Gerald Murnane

The man who believed
that televised weather forecasts
make it all happen:

the woman who did all her foreign travel
under a lemon tree
in her backyard, with an atlas:

the young man, faintly adventurous,
who entered a maze and never came out,
leaving a handkerchief behind:

the cabin attendant, or trolley-dolly,
afflicted by her entirely terrible
fear of heights:

the country butcher
whose father falling blind drunk
had been gobbled up by pigs:

the teenage girl whose main belief was that, if she fell
asleep, her legs
and arms might easily drop off:

the little boy who felt at night
the surrounding darkness
was all made of water

and the chubby rose-pink baby
who had remembered it all
but now forgot

The Speech of Birds

That there should now
be red berries down there
to the left of third-big-tree
will concern me later

for now I know
plentiful grass-seeds are eating-ready
near fence and far enough
from cat

and even before that
I'll pick up
those excellent lengths of straw
just the shot

for home repairs
a bit closer though
to big cat prowling ground

Four legs more dangerous
two more or less benign
but upstairs in our tree

those bloody wattlebirds
and squealing gangs of lorikeets
could drive one crazy

Some days I can't even hear
a melodious lovesong
from down the way

nor the clamant warning
that sparrowhawk is hovering now
somewhere above leafless

riding the breath of death

At the Bionic Elephant

But the very, ticking, universe
is a hydraulic jiggermetite
run by the corporate remains
of Newton's horologist god,

He or She or probably it
cranking the pressure up and up.
The steel articulated trunk
will curl when children turn a wheel:

Ganesh in joints of carbon steel.

Molecules turning inside my gut
combine to chorus coffee-time:
a left rear knee is daintily raised.
To every action – entropy;

to every good intention, what?
Oil doesn't flow to the squeaky wheel
except in some academy.
This hayty-ho is hollow, though.

Casuarinas drooping outside
are wryly where they need to be,
culture following in nature's train,
but these four limbs are jointed steel:

a small girl winds another wheel.

It's terribly mortal now, in here,
summer snoozing along outside.
This is the jumbo that doesn't sway
nor take the kiddies for a ride.

Since we all fear the natural
a beast that's powered like this delights
a hunger in us.
                Metal shines,
part of a timely, shitless universe,

attractive as the tall tales of sci-fi.
No sin haunts this quadruped
nor sliding taint of relativity.
Our cool museum stands for mind

and every action's fixity.

Do I Sleep or Am I Slept?

At morning there came the dream that includes all dreams,
its detail unclear, but mastery quite profound;
with no visible characters
                    it owned all the pigeonholes:
the future was eaten away.

Perhaps it was the Word.
Needing no breath of syntax it reached out,
imposing domination on the first
                    half of my ordinary Sunday.

Clearly it had prejudged
parking spot, dates, tennis booking, proper names
just when that bill was due.
                    Design! Design!

On top of my questions, the answer lay
like an old cat.

Celestial timber, silent joinery,
the universe had been fitted out with shelves
on my behalf.

A Faun's Arvo

Memory is a curious organ
and can be inflated, as you know
or half-know,
however language tries to tie it down.

When there was no There
Lilith or Sheba came,
preceding even the name of the game,
so the brain obliquely remembers,
and the limbs do.

Her ghost stirs smokily underneath
our muscle and human breath.

Somewhere at full midnight then
the grass has been thoroughly trodden down;
there are horse-tracks in the sand.

Those nymphs, I'd like to put them in a film,
the other poet said about all this,
bees murmuring in a ripeness
through his eclogue,
making nothing happen once again.

Listen! The shape of hooves
lost in your blood.

Meanings of Lowell

'There mounts in squalls a sort of rusty mire'

For us, back in the fifties, American poetry
Meant Robert Lowell. When young we had absorbed
Eliot, Pound and fastidious John Ransom,
Flirted a little maybe at frigid Tate;
Moore and Stevens were still too hard for us
But along came this percussive Milton
Thundering off mysterious Nantucket
And giving God a good talking-to
In His own voice – or that of the prophets.

I remember flyting at a boozy party
Alternate sections of the 'Quaker Graveyard'
With a swarthy Welsh poet, long since gone.
A few other poems grabbed us by the scruff
Of the neck or the seat of our pants.
'Falling Asleep over the Aeneid'
Taunted us, paramount among all these
For its cunning use of what Jesperson calls
'Preparatory there' down that winding staircase
Of grammar filled with writhing solids
Defining some weird Hôtel de Ville;
Curious, too, was Lowell's use of negation
Telling us what we would not see.

His family portraits, revealing life
In grainy diurnal realism
(Releasing us all into self-absorption)
Were to come a few years later
And years of teaching I had from them, too:
All that stuff inaugurated the sixties.

At last I met Cal at Jarrell's wake,
If a wake can actually be formal
And held in panelled New Haven. He stood stooped,
Remarkably tall, with a head like a boulder
And grave Bostonian courtesy;
He yarned a bit about Siddy Nolan
But largely was intrigued
By Asia's dangling over Australia
And why we weren't scared shitless of China.
I guess he must always have brooded on war.

Near the Ha-Ha, Bundanon

Out of some gaunt yarn of troll or dragon
the claws of scarlet begin to fantail out
at the raggedy twig-tips,
all these writhingly sinuous flame trees
putting on late winter flaunt and aggro,
ignored, of course, by the noisy miners,
busy sweeping all other birds away.

There are no cats on this cool avian catwalk:
over the manicured buffalo grass,
trampoline-soft with a texture akin
to Stanley Spencer's rendered Harris tweed,
satin bowerbirds are cock-a-hooping with
their unbelievably tasteful wives
shopping, no doubt, for something to take home.

The long hillcrests are handwriting
on a whiteboard constructed from pale blue,
their olive ink dripping straight down
into the unseen river, roughly where
yellow-clumpy wattle dots and speckles
our wombat-modest margins of expectation,

just beyond those quizzical kangaroos.

Leaning Against the Golden Undertow

for Dimitris Tsaloumas

Mutely I wish
they were still heartbreaking Chopin yet
there is a sense
in which all things take place but once
as one small glass
of Italian brandy runs bland to my head
or frostblades green
quite suddenly. Named ones who die by
fire or gunfire
have their names wiped clean off the blackboard:
memory's tears
retain them a little but scuffed sand is replaned
by each high tide;
moon and water prove eloquent saddest of all because
they masquerade
like that Hampstead nightingale not to be born for death
and eat our hearts,
those muscular pumps which do not mind at all
being fickle
or wise, or just a wee bit hopeful
as cloud veils moon
and arpeggios of shaken saltwater darken
only to soon
re-point themselves with rhinestones and silvery flecks.
We think this helps.
Teasers and dreams, wrote the old ambiguist
so I chop these logs to prove I still exist.

Intermezzo

There is an interval, a patch or crest
round about seven, when those Bay breezes deign
to press on this far inland for a while
over the hot parked cars, parched side gardens and
young men ambling slowly nowhere much
slangily along the asphalt just beyond
our healthy, red-rimmed, thick photinia hedge
behind which I genuinely can
dry myself in the morning, naked as an egg,
much as though holidaying by the surf
in ambiguous diminished summers which
I had in tan days, or used to have.

This drought-pale year even the fruit bats
have gone AWOL, for some unreason:
no longer tempted by the loitering apricots
of which we had loads too many. Every lawn or grass patch
crossed these mornings I inspect with scrupulous care,
like a troubled botanist, or like
some historian of the great Apocalypse:
a world finally too tired of our mob
marking all this by that early-seeded straw.

Birds change their habits, as the bourgeois do.
Swimming-pools fall dry, tree-feeders take now
to picking up their pickings on the ground
and why were those two familial magpies
skulking there under a miniature cypress tree?
They looked like quaint ceramics.

Around midnight it could well be soothing
to pour Cinzano Rosso onto chunks of ice,
stroking the mind alive. But in the upshot
(What on earth is an upshot, by the way?)

I could just as well dunk my sweaty self
into a still cold bath. Or do neither
but slummock around.

Scroll down
to a stuffy dawn uneasily, the stumptailed cat
disconcerted by a ceiling fan failing
to be a bird. I do hear a rooster somewhere.

Time for a cup of tea in bed, or on it,
and preparing defences against the long day ahead,

breathing air like cotton-wool.

Parking for Zeno

Corner of P and N, early in the century. Two people come stooping out of a car and whang the doors shut. They have used it to arrive at P from... elsewhere. A cherry-red sedan, Japanese, it cools on bluestone cobbles, the blocks here inexorably nudged up by tentacles of English elm. Another import, once. The two, scrawny youth and blanched woman, go into a milkwhite terrace where a stranger will tell them something utterly different. The bell coughs. Carpeted footsteps pad. They fade, hand in hand, through that open door, their curiously streaky future closing over like cloud. There is a low-pressure system moving in from the Bight. Sheep weather alert. This time will never come flowing again, and nothing, in its peculiar way, is happening to us all.

The Stone's in the Midst of All

for Vincent O'Sullivan

Little by little
things have been passing over me,
liquid, furry, ephemeral
slowcoach aeons and banks of cloud.

There have been good and bad millennia
according to some principle or other.

Sometimes I shift a bit
but mostly just lie around
while happening happens to others
who then go away.
                    Soon enough:
it's hard to know what they were there for.

So here I am
                    and abide
taking things pretty much as they come,
different from the fickle weather,
set in my ways but
gaining a certain polish.

And our speculative humans, lairy
with all their bundles of hubbub,
                    their brief diversity,
drift clean away.

Remember those worthy Neanderthals?
Gone with the long wind.

A Descendant

I fancy I'm descended from the Picts
But we don't appear to know much about those painterly people,
Least of all what lingo they might have been speaking
Rattling on in the cold, all those poor savages
With, I like to imagine, a St Andrews accent, better still an
                                                    Aberdonian
Because they now employ the best English of all,
Unless the Barbadians do. Which is another matter,
And somehow related to cannonball fast bowling.

Our patrilineal family came from the crumbled heart
Of traditional Pictish country, close enough
To their curious dark stones marooned in a Christian churchyard,
Not that they'd have known a Pict from a Skraeling,
Most of them.
                    In fact, much as those tattooed tribesmen of yore
(I like to pop in a phrase like 'of yore', don't you?)
Cobbled up their disgraceful invasion scheme with the Saxons,
Black Geordie, my grandpa, hurried off south of the border,
Failing to reinvent the past – until he sailed out here.

A bit of a pity there are parish records
Otherwise we could knit any brand of past at all:
Once here, for example, he became a kilted highlander
At the drop of a hat, or discreet swirl of a kilt.

We'd be utterly ignorant about those mythical Picts
If it weren't for my favourite Latin author,
Whose quite astonishing sleight of voice was to give us
The persuasive speaking voice of a Pictish chieftain,
Who may well be quoted more
Than any other soul from bonnie Scotland,
At least for the next eighteen-hundred years.

After all, there's always Robbie Burns.

I don't know how far I'm going to get
With all those blessed Picts, bar the fact that we
All are hungry about distant origins, micropoetically located
In the fog between Brothers Grimm and DNA,
But having anything Gaelic at all about you
Can be swanky, or else a continuing pain in the kilt.

But there you are, then, all of us need a mythology;
So, for the general sake of my vitamins
I fancy that I'm descended from the Picts.

One Step after Another

Could it be
that our trailing lives are seen
by the perhaps god
as being sweet and brief
like the first scent of summer rain?

It's that last wriggle
on feet of sand
as you ease off
wet bathers
under a sarong-like beach towel
without showing off
all your goodies.

Tesserae much like this
apparently, alas,
make up a life:
there's no getting away from it.

When you come to realise
that God is not the answer
but the question
then you are on your way
to wise confusion
or even to humility,

apologising too
for all that sand on the lino floor.

Reading Smoke with Orpheus

after Poussin

Tranquillity. It can be painted, but
it's very much like reading smoke
or seeing a snake as mobile typography.

Gods ruling the dark and wordless world,
everyone born of woman comes to you;
        you are the debtors we have to pay,
        even a musician must in time
                        shell out.

Orpheus lolled in his deckchair, strumming the lute.
His wife screamed, but music does not hear
        the sound of lesser sounds
        and so the venom struck,
        the bud was plucked
before her flower so much as came to flower

                since everything arrives
                and goes too soon.

What is the use of grief? It's only
a blind wind sowing the sand with sand;
and so is music, if it comes to that,
        which it always does,
since even Joseph Haydn's cunning harmonies
are beaten up by destiny.

Yet the underworld
            is not an overlord,
more like your shadow on the well-mown
                                        grass.

The towers burn, the paysage is perfection:
art for a while, after all,
keeps fingernails of the macnads well away
and a head on your shoulders.

How still the waters,
unshaken those neoclassical trees.

Provincial Distinctions

In just the same way
must the odd group of, say,
Libyans or Cappadocians
have sat back at ease around
gourmet cooking, modest local wine,
with music and smiling and large
communication in the air
to harp at their dearest topic:
They have no sense of humour.
They're terribly slow-witted
and their women unspeakable.
The elephants will smash them to bits;
that or the German guerrillas.

Views bouncing to and fro
loudly, hospitably
in the same chatterbox way
off cobbles and rudely painted stucco,
opinions without a hearing
in dusty Italy.

Boleyn, Tourist

Dear stinking city, such a hive
of shoulder-wrenching power play
            and loose heads,
so I won the endgame, after all,
and the silken skirts of my daughter
are flaring out across a chequered kingdom.

Oh yes,
        the city becomes pure extension:
        it is all milk, it grows mother-of-pearl,
blazing water and eye-watering light
over to the dock-pocked shore
and cruel Tower, softened like china-clay.

        The self knows no bounds at all,
        connected to violent eternity
        by tranquil passages
        of some disembodied pigment.

        But London throbs with morning.

Illumination carries me away
ripping a mortal grid apart, the sometime flesh,
and thus dunking poor old self
in the silken
texture of never dying at all, being one of the gods
in the long, dazzled run.

Mozart on the Road

'the sensibility of his organs appears to have been excessive'
The Book of Days

Too much of his childhood
would have been bumped and sloshed away
in a post chaise or damp coach
between indescribable towns
or jammed into yet another
unsewered inn. Not good

for a bright boy growing up.
What could he have been doing
on the slow road between, say,
Schitzberg and Krappfeld?
Would he and Nannerl have found
word games to make up?

It must all have played
merry hell with his constitution,
yet his mind worked away
like a Stakhanovite
through many a traffic jam
or when some new board displayed

notice that the bridge
not far ahead was down.
And what did he take for his colds?
Did Leopold bring a flask
of eau-de-vie? All such travel
was far from a privilege.

Travel narrows the mind,
one is often tempted to say,
but he was quick as a flash,
impressions through muddy windows
metamorphosing into
harmonies unconfined

by the curiosity
of rude, stinking, scruffy postilions.
All this flowed into a thought-voice
which evoked such terrible yearning
that nothing but itself
could ever satisfy.

The Drudges

Poets on the circuit
stay at small hotels:
nothing in the fridge there
but exhausted smells.

Poets on the circuit
divert some tiny crowd.
If your verse is vapid
better declaim it loud.

Poets on the circuit
are talking out their days.
As they won't get money,
all they need is praise.

Poets on the circuit
have shocks of silver hair.
Yes, they'll do a reading
more or less anywhere.

A Triptych for my Father

1

When he came back from the War
he still wore the soft
greyish blue of the British
Air Force, not our darkblue
(he had been too old for ours)

and my little brother whispered,
That man's here still, in the cold
morning, unable to
assimilate this return
from the fabulous, curried East
far to our north, far up
the Eurocentric map
which Dad had fought to maintain
in face of the sweat and sprawl
of Japanese marauding.

When Dad flew in from the War
our world was perfectly
old, firewoody, dinkum,
the iceman's weeping truck
still dawdling down warm streets
and a Chinese greengrocer
obscurely urging his horse
another few short yards.

2

It was my Dad's old chum
from the Burma Rifles.
He said the very best time
was up on the North-West Frontier.
We looked out through a moist Sussex window,
sipping a whisky each.

He told me about the dangers
of the International Jew,
knowing playfully well of course
that I didn't approve one bit,
then wheeling back again
to dusty days on the Khyber Pass.
There hadn't been any real trouble
with the Pathans at all:
'We ran an electric fence
round the whole bang lot of them.'
You could tell he sort of believed it,
like he did the story about
Julius Caesar's dog.

3

Father, you were able to praise
whatever I did, or had a shot at:
educationally creaky
but nourishing in the long, brisk haul,
you dear old bloke.
Enthusiastic you were
as a Baptist or March hare;
a bloke could feel bloody good
leaning on your support,
stocky Jack-of-all-skills.
Dad, you did richly so much
to fashion me how I am
but you're sixteen years gone under.
Ashen ripples inside me could well be
all that heaven can mean,
the grit of resurrection
puffing briefly
                    on the west wind.
That's what I love, the take-off,
an exalted thrumming of pressure
as the big turtle races on,
faster and ever faster.

Not Going to Korea After All

Every morning, a little after sparrowfart
we shuffled onto the bullring
                in boiler suit and blue cunt cap,
the flight sergeant wearily barking.

One rookie became a popeyed star of the telly,
another contrived to keep his job as a butcher
by nicking out through the wire.
                One summery day

in the pale dust of country roads
three of us broke the four-minute mile:
the speedo must have been crook.
                I kept marching
my platoon in oblongs to pass the prettiest WAAF.

We had radio classes, were bored quite shitless,
read the new Penguin Classics:
                Flaubert, cool Chekhov
and cluey pseudonymous Stendhal. Right there.

Our dirtiest talker was really called Mike Hunt;
wind and gravel began to pall,
lights of the city ever more
                seductive, until

six months were clean gone. We had served
our country. Beaut.
                Time to get back into
vitello parmigian' at the downstairs Hoddle,

a beer strike, and what they call Real Life.

The World as Will and Idea

I

Is it the being older
　　and, in my general suntan,
failure to realise
　　quite how the slippery

decades have stripped my cells
　　or substituted
those of lower octane
　　that makes me romantic?

Unduly frivolous
　　in shorts, not a grey suit,
I steadfastly become the one
　　whom I pretend to be.

II

You're quite correct, Tom Hardy,
we cannot see the future,
a time beyond our death

because the person we insert
is a present self only,
never the self-of-then.

We think of it like tourists
waiting for their planetary ship.

A Summons in the Peak Period

A phone is ringing in the cemetery
loud enough to be from the Resurrection.

You can hear it over busy morning traffic
where the living drive to work, or merely shopping.

Not a soul appears to have heard the summons,
but maybe they're all sick to death of phonecalls.

It's very loud; probably needs to be.
The majority have slept there for a while.

Still, what if this were a long-distance call,
God calling collect from Paradise?

Through cypress fingers and elegant ironbarks
it keeps on ringing, grossly magnified

so that nobody fails to get the point.
It surely disturbed those paint-bright lorikeets

and brand-name kids dragging across to school.
The call might just have been from grandma,

or even for her.
Hello? Hello?
                    There's nobody awake.

Stranger Country

'Something is missing inside us which makes us what we are.'

Terry Eagleton

They stagger or drip
    in metaphysical space,
nature abolished like a heap of kindling
or bomber target Wadi X

because this barren spot is
not merely an ending of the world,

but theologically beyond all that,
a comic book of cancelled revelations
wrecked upon yellow dunes.

There waits no medicine for being human,
it's terminal and thus hilarious:
anxiety takes them all by the hand
                at least for now.

Dust in the eye-corners:
inert gases where the soul should reside.

        Because they are also us,
judgement sways and falters
old ligaments tightening up,
limping in our long, subjective jogathon
round the desolate park

for now.

The Land of Motionless Childhood

Funny phrases, the oldies had in stock.
'Treat him with the ignore he deserves',
my Dad would say, then head into the dunny
for a smoke, too often leaving a butt
floating unsightly there, like a German sub.

I'm talking about postwar days then,
after ration books were over, and their shiny scissors
dangling on short string; well over,
but our Mum could still stage-whisper,
'Tell your little friends to go home now, dear.'

'And use a hankyfish, don't sniff', she might go on
before a calming smoke in the living room
beside her beloved piano. So she spent
a helluva lot of her time on her pat malone.
Were we much help to her? Like fun we were:

what with block battles and Biggles books
we'd muck around in the woolly bedroom
hatching history; or else nick off to play
cricket in the street. Every kid knew,
those days, how to make use of a street.

We'd throw brinnies at cars, then scamper away
if some angry nude-nut stopped and clambered out.
Fear was part of the point of things, back then.
Later, we would ride our bikes down to St Kilda
on the sweaty look-out for sweater girls;

if we spotted one we didn't even whistle,
but sort of knew it was a world like magazines.
One girl on the tram was a real sort;
one on the second tram was rumoured to Do It –
with oafish boys from the First Eighteen.

Now get that down your little red lane,
I'd get told, cornered, chewing away
at the last grey wad of roast beef. We didn't
say 'Yuk', yet, but some guru did it
in that comic, 'The Katzenjammer Kids'.

I was a slowcoach like the iceman's trickling truck
but something or other went on filtering in.
Pity was played out in the pattern of words,
Doctor Spooner conducting behind our tears
his harmony of puns and consonants.

Loving in Truth

Someone will push the house over one day,
Some spacedozer give it a shove,
But the cobbles we laid down here in the yard,
These are a labour of love.

All winter we set these cobbles in place,
Or was it the summer as well?
Sorting through lumpy bluestone pitchers
For ones that looked suitable.

The old house decayed – along with us –
Will a strange new resident
Admire the patio made in joy
Wondering what we meant?

Things fall apart, the poet wrote,
Certainties crumble and move
But the cobbles oddly plotted together,
These are our labour of love.

Oh Yes, Then

When I am rotting patiently where
my eldest, Ben, now lies
and the bright prunus petals are dropping away
faster than flies,

when Georgia has swatches of grey
in her falls of fairish hair,
Toby has a neat condominium
set up offshore somewhere,

and a nimbler, wiser Josh outdoors
is performative with his hands,
busy as a rock-cod, making something
he tacitly understands,

where will you be, the flamingly
joyous hearth of my heart?
I can't get the answer, no matter how
I tune up the shawms of art.

We Are All Grown-ups

What is your music made of?
the golden retriever asked the hunter
who blinked and replied,
What is the name of a smell?

Silence
        and the heedless rabbit loped away
        into its blackberry tangle.

Selected titles from the Oxford*Poets* list

Oxford*Poets*, an imprint of Carcanet Press, celebrates the vitality and diversity of contemporary poetry in English.

Joseph Brodsky *Collected Poems in English*
For Brodsky, to be a poet was an absolute, a total necessity...scintillating deployment of language, and always tangential or odd ways of interpreting ideas, events or other literature. John Kinsella, OBSERVER

Greg Delanty *Collected Poems 1986–2006*
A body of work that has grown steadily from book to book in depth, invention, and ambition. AGENDA

Jane Draycott *The Night Tree*
Hers is a scrupulous intelligence...Her searching curiosity and wonderful assurance make her an impeccable and central poetic intelligence. Penelope Shuttle, MANHATTAN REVIEW

Sasha Dugdale *The Estate*
Dugdale creates a spare, mythical tone that fits itself perfectly to the elemental Russian landscape in which much of her collection is set. GUARDIAN

Rebecca Elson *A Responsibility to Awe*
This is a wise and haunting volume, which I can't recommend too warmly. Boyd Tonkin, INDEPENDENT

Marilyn Hacker *Essays on Departure*
Everything is thrilling and true, fast and witty, deep and wise; her vitality is the pulse of life itself. Derek Mahon

Peter Scupham *Collected Poems*
The sophistication of the technique which underpins every poem becomes clearer and clearer as you read further in this substantial, generous, distinguished volume. Peter Davidson, Books of the Year 2005, READYSTEADYBOOK.COM

Charles Tomlinson *Cracks in the Universe*
Tomlinson is a unique voice in contemporary English poetry, and has been a satellite of excellence for the past 50 years. David Morley, GUARDIAN

Marina Tsvetaeva *Selected Poems*, trans. **Elaine Feinstein**
Feinstein has performed the first, indispensable task of a great translator: she has captured a voice. THREEPENNY REVIEW

Chris Wallace-Crabbe *By and Large*
His allies are words, and he sues them with the care of a surgeon and the flair of a conjuror. Peter Porter

---

Visit **www.carcanet.co.uk** to browse a complete list of Oxford*Poets* and Carcanet titles, find out about forthcoming books and order books at discounted prices.

Email **info@carcanet.co.uk** to subscribe to the Carcanet e-letter for poetry news, events and a poem of the week.